WE CRY

ALEX STEPHENSON

HOUSE CAT BOOKS

ISBN: 978-1-64446-028-3

Illustrated by Gastrasion.

1 3 5 7 9 8 6 4 2

Printed in the United States
Published by

R
Rowe Publishing
www.rowepub.com

To Chris and Dalton

We cry because we're happy.

We cry because we're sad.

We cry when things get scary.

We cry when things are over.

We cry when things begin.

We cry to be let out sometimes.

We cry to be let in.

ARRIVALS

We cry when we're together.

We cry when we're alone.

We cry when we are little.

We cry when we are grown.

We cry when we have lost someone.

We cry because they're gone.

We cry when we remember.

We cry to carry on.

We cry when we are hurting.

We cry to help us heal.

We cry because it's ok.

We cry because we feel.

www.ingramcontent.com/pod-product-compliance
Lightning Source LLC
Chambersburg PA
CBRC092219080325
22968CB00001BA/1